Saving the Young Men of Vienna

The Brittingham·Prize in Poetry

THE UNIVERSITY OF WISCONSIN PRESS POETRY SERIES

RONALD WALLACE, GENERAL EDITOR

Saving the Young Men of Vienna

DAVID KIRBY

The University of Wisconsin Press

Published 1987

The University of Wisconsin Press
114 North Murray Street
Madison, Wisconsin 53715

The University of Wisconsin Press, Ltd.
1 Gower Street
London WC1E 6HA, England

First printing

Printed in the United States of America

For LC CIP information see the colophon

ISBN 0–299–11220–9 cloth; 0–299–11224–1 paper

For Barbara, Will, and Ian

To invent is to choose.

—Henri Poincaré,
"Mathematical Creation"

Contents

Foreword

Tired of the stingy poems which issue forth in their thousands from a stale, far-too-long-ago-"received" minimalism? Those which some of us categorize as the "I wake up this morning and look out of the window and I see . . ." poems, in which a brief listing of what the poet's eye happens to fall upon makes up his total gift to the reader? (Or its corollary, the "I wake up this morning and I feel? . . . ," followed by a list of the moment's emotions?) Weary of the assumption behind such offerings: that the writer need never *earn*, through traditional or experimental resources of language, the reader's intense interest in any random detail of his inner or outer self? Here, for your reading pleasure, is a more generous poet.

In a perpetually attractive group of paintings, the incompatible beasts of the world are compelled by the artistry of the brush to lie down together. For as long as the viewer gazes within the frame, so great is the earned complicity between artist and audience, he submits to that illusion of harmonious quiescence. The experience refreshes him long afterward, when confusing and irreconcilable elements revert to the fierceness or feebleness of their own nature. In "The Peaceable Kingdom" of a David Kirby poem the framing of an identifiable voice and a strong, encompassing closure brings and binds together the paradoxical, the funny, the sad, the messy, the precious in aesthetic concord. His palette is brighter and braver for its inclusion of the often-scanted hues of statements, idea, vivacity of language and an interest in beings beyond the self. His audience will surely be refreshed by a view which is so fundamentally affectionate.

MONA VAN DUYN
1987 Judge, Brittingham Prize

Acknowledgments

Some of these poems appeared first in *Amelia*, *Apalachee Quarterly*, *Carolina Quarterly*, *Chattahoochee Review*, *Chelsea*, *Florida Review*, *Indiana Review*, *Jam To-Day*, *Kansas Quarterly*, *Light Year '86*, *Mid-American Review*, *Negative Capability*, *New Mexico Humanities Review*, *Pendragon*, *Ploughshares*, *The Quarterly*, *Queen's Quarterly*, *Round Table*, *Southern Humanities Review*, and *Southern Poetry Review*.

"Unnatural Acts" and "Conversations with the Dead" won the 1983 *Kansas Quarterly* First Poetry Award.

"I Think I Am Going to Call My Wife Paraguay" won the 1985 Guy Owen Poetry Prize from *Southern Poetry Review*.

An earlier version of "Saving the Young Men of Vienna" appeared in *Sarah Bernhardt's Leg* (Cleveland State Poetry Center, 1983).

The writing of these poems was made possible by grants from the Florida Arts Council and the National Endowment for the Arts and a sabbatical from Florida State University.

Saving the Young Men of Vienna

Man Drowning in Restaurant

A man is drowning in a crowded restaurant.
Something about his meal upset him,
and he wanted to cry, but he was afraid
that the other customers would make fun of him,
so now he is filling up with his own tears.
Waitresses hurry past with cups of soup
and slices of pâté, plates of chicken and fish,
ice cream and coffee, while the drowning man
struggles to free himself from his light brown jacket
and cream shantung shirt, tries to kick off
his dark trousers, his brown and white shoes.

He is an embarrassment to his friends.
He will have to drop his club memberships,
his fiancée will break with him,
and almost certainly he will lose his job,
but right now he is trying so hard to reach
the pure air near the ceiling
that he cannot begin to say what it is
that upset him so in the first place;
to drown has become his *raison d'être*.

The other customers continue to eat;
either everything is to their satisfaction
or they know better than to take disappointment
to heart. The drowning man wants them to notice
how well he drowns, but now they are putting on
their coats and unwrapping the little mints
the waitresses have given them along with their checks.
In the half-light of the empty restaurant
the drowning man looks like a dancer
doing something difficult but beautiful
and useless, something to live for.

The New Barber

The new barber circles my head,
cursing under his breath:
"Aw, crap," he says
as his scissors come together,
then, "Damn it!"
He will not last.
I will not turn him in,
but the other customers will complain:
"That new barber curses,"
they'll say,
"he uses swear words."
I hope the old barbers
will explain the situation,
point out that all of us
are frustrated by our jobs.
Maybe they will tell him
not to be so hard on himself,
not to set goals
that are unattainable.

Leaving the shop,
I see a couple
getting out of a car,
but they do not walk ten feet
before stopping to have words:
the wife tells her husband
to drop dead and walks away.
My father still thinks
I am clever and can find things
that are lost,
but I am not clever
and have to ask my own son

to find things for me.
Sometimes he does.
Sometimes he doesn't.
I want to go
back to the shop and say,
listen, we are all new barbers here.

In Praise of Sausage

The sun will not rise for an hour,
and the only sound in the kitchen
is the hiss of grease on hot metal
as I put another patty of sausage
into the pan. I am half-asleep and dreaming,
and what comes to mind does so in no order:
the slope of my wife's breasts;
a photo of my father,
stooped and white but smiling,
soon to go before me into the Great Mystery;
the cashier at the supermarket
where I bought the sausage, saying,
"Thank you for not wearing any underpants,
and have a nice day."
Outside the moon is so bright
you can see your shadow. From the window
I watch myself fall out of the night sky,
toward the ground-up things of the world.

I Think I Am Going to Call My Wife Paraguay

I think I am going to call my wife Paraguay,
for she is truly bilingual,
even though she speaks no Guaraní
and, except for "cucaracha" and "taco,"
hardly any Spanish at all.
She has two zones, though,
one a forest luxuriant with orchids
and the smell of fruit trees,
where the Indians worship
the pure and formless Tupang,
who shines in the lightning
and roars in the thunder,
the other a dry plain,
a flat place with the soul of a mountain,
motionless and hard as a rock.
During the day the sun blazes
on the red dust of Paraguay
as dark-eyed, straight-backed women
walk home from the river
with bundles of laundry on their heads,
hoping to avoid trouble,
for the Paraguayans are always fighting;
young conscripts lolling in faded cotton uniforms
have no idea whether they will be summoned next
to overthrow the government or defend it.
My wife Paraguay and I
ourselves had to fight the War of the Triple Alliance,
although in our case
it wasn't Brazil, Uruguay, and Argentina
but Harry, Edward, and Maurice,
her former boyfriends. I won.
War does not silence Paraguay
or dismay her in any way,

for still her people shout on the football fields
and whisper declarations of love
on the darkened patios of the old colonial houses,
just as my wife Paraguay says that she loves me
as the parroquet and toucan fly over
and the perfume of the lime and orange tree
blow through the windows of our big house,
which I call South America
because it contains Paraguay
and is shaped like a sweet potato.

The Disappearance

There is a man in a tea room
in Bath who is saying that
all he wants is a little peace,
and another man, presumably
his son-in-law, is assuring him
that that's what he has,
and the older man is saying
that that's what he wants,
but it isn't really what he wants
because he keeps saying it
over and over again until
the tea room in Bath fills
with his quiet, angry voice
as the other customers
eat quickly and call for
their checks, his voice
following them out into the street
where it cracks with rage
and self-pity but is silenced
at last by voices quieter still
that speak of other things,
of the man who stumbled
into the cave where Arthur
lay sleeping, only to flee,
never finding his way back,
when the king woke
and asked simply, "Is it time?"
or the apparition of the angel
over Mons as the soldiers
marched into battle,

dismissed as an effect
of light and cloud by skeptics
but not by the ones who were there,
who said if only
you could have heard it singing.

Amazed by Chekhov

Whenever I see a production
of *Wild Honey*, say, or *The Seagull*,
I want to run up on stage
and drink vodka with the characters I admire
and knock the villains down
and have all the women throw themselves at my feet.
I forget that the people up there
are just actors who would probably freeze
or hurry off as the curtain came down
and that I would be hustled away by understudies,
eager nobodies destined for nothing better
than television commercials, if they're lucky,
but trying now to impress the stars
by the force with which they hurl me into the alley,
where I bruise and cut myself and tear my clothes.
As for my wife, well!
There would be a study in anger for you!
"You've embarrassed me for the last time,"
she'd say, and that would be the end of,
not a perfect marriage, but a good one nonetheless.
On the other hand, maybe the players would say,
"Marvellous! Wonderful! You're here at last,
old man! Have a drink!"
                                And that would be my life:
I'd spend the rest of my days acting my heart out
and getting these huge rounds of applause.
I would have to say the same thing over and over again,
but at least it would be brilliant.
And even though something terrible would happen to me
sooner or later, that's simply the price
that would have to be paid by a character
as well-loved as mine. Then *quoi faire?*
as one of Chekhov's impoverished Francophiles would say.
How's this: to get up some evening

when the jokes and the non sequiturs
are flying around like crazy
and make my way to the end of the aisle
as if to go for an ice cream or the bathroom
and get a running start
and fly up the steps
with a big stupid grin on my face
and just disappear into the light.

A Town Called Mere

There is a little bread
on the plate
and, in the cup,
some tea, about a spoonful—
that's what they have
for breakfast in Mere,
and as for the paper,
it's down the street,
in the yard
of someone
who will glance at it
indifferently, if at all,
because deliveries
never quite make it
to the front door here,
and no one cares if they do;
packages are left
in the driveway
to be run over
and rained on,
and the milk sours
under the dead azaleas.
When the people of Mere
come home from work,
having done nothing,
they sometimes despair
of reaching their own doors
and simply lie down
in a car
or under one,
if all the cars are full,
or in a field
whose name

no one remembers.
No one is ever born
in Mere;
last year, a man
took his wife's hand
in his own for a moment
and let it drop.
Yet no one dies, either:
no one worries
himself to death,
and the people are too lazy
to kill.
And no one leaves:
after all, Heaven
to the people of Mere
would be Mere,
and Hell would be down the road a way,
a little town called Splendid.

Crustacea

*Darwin's study of barnacles extended over eight years, 1846 to 1854.
In his systematic way of working he generally set aside two and a half
hours each day for the barnacles. This became so much a part of the
family routine that one of his children assumed that this was what
grownup men did and asked the children of another household, "When
does your father do his barnacles?"*
　　　　　　　—GEORGE GAYLORD SIMPSON, *The Book of Darwin*

The Neighbor's Eldest Child

Our father does his barnacles in a somewhat
irregular manner, devoting himself to them for hours
on end and then allowing two weeks or more to pass
without giving them so much as a glance. But though
he does not do them nearly so well as Mr. Darwin does
his, nonetheless he takes such pleasure in his studies
that we not only indulge but emulate his example,
though we prefer quoits and pitchpenny to shellfish.
By "our" I mean the father of the nine of us, including
Charlotte and Edward, deceased.

The Neighbor Observed

No, no, no. Hmmm . . . ahhh . . . I—hmmm . . .
no . . . I wonder . . . yes . . . I . . . ahh, that's . . .
hmmmmmm . . . blast!

Charlotte and Edward, Looking Down on Their Father's Exertions

We have learned with regret that, in the process
of doing his barnacles, our father has lost his

traditional beliefs, becoming a non- but not clearly
an anti-Christian, from there passing through a period
of non-Christian theism, and ending in a nearly but
not completely atheistic agnosticism. We neither
complain nor disapprove, though we regret that
he does not share our view or expect confidently to
enjoy an immortal afterlife with us.

We died young, by which time we had absorbed,
at our mother's knee, a belief in the hereafter as
perdurable as the chalk flats on which our father's
house is situated. Perhaps it is well that we did
not live to do our barnacles as he does his, for the
doing of them would have knocked our belief on the
head, and clearly it is our belief that has brought us
to this most pleasant place.

The Song of the Barnacles

*P*auvres us!
We are the order Cirrepedia
and kin to all barnacles,
yet different

from those of Darwin
because *nous ne savons pas*
when we are going
to be studied.

For Darwin's lot,
it's clockwork:
two and a half hours
each day.

How know we this?
Très simple:
Their brine
is our brine.

The Neighbor's Wife, But Not without Bitterness

For some months there was a serving girl who would
sit on my husband's lap and kiss him, but that was all.
She seemed baffled by the things he hissed at her: his
raptures, his declarations of devotion, his promises to
divorce me and take her away to Italy. I knew and
said nothing. Eventually she became frightened and
ran away. He turned to science. Though his research
is fitful, I must say he is trying very hard. Everyone
should have a hobby.

The Neighbor's Eldest Child Again

Let's face it, these are nervous times. Small
wonder that Mr. Dickens, up in London, and after him
Mr. Robert Louis Stevenson, will grow rich from their
pen-portraits of the divided self. Here at home the
emphasis is on being sensible and not running out to
play until your dinner goes down. A boy at school
says his aunt threatened to punish him by hanging his
cat. The constable came, but most of the townspeople
say this was an overreaction; the cat scratched the
aunt and ran beneath the sofa, where he has been ever
since. Also, I don't notice anyone going out of his
way to answer *my* questions.

The Late News

The anchorwoman is unsmiling, even somber,
for her biggest stories are about death,
and even when she has a feature
on a twelve-year-old college student
or a gorilla who understands sign language,
there is something tentative about her relief:
she knows that the Great Antagonist
will strike again, and soon.

The weatherman smiles a lot,
but he is making the best of a bad thing,
for the weather is necessary, yes,
but boring. As for the actors
in the commercials, they are jovial
yet insincere, for they do not love the lotions,
sprays, and gargles they urge us to buy,
products that are bad for us anyway and overpriced.

Only the sportscaster is happy, for sports news
is good news: money always changes hands,
and if someone has lost that day, someone else has won.
Should anyone die, that's death, not sports,
and death is the anchorwoman's department.
Even if the Soviets should fire all their missiles at us
and vice versa, the sportscaster will still be happy:
you can't cover everything in a half hour,

for crissakes, and sports will be all that is left.
There will be no jobs to go to, and our cars won't work,
and there will be no electricity,
but you can make a ball out of anything,
and then all you need is a line to get it across
or a hoop to put it through. The sportscaster knows
how the world will end: not with a whimper,
not with a bang, but with a cheer.

The Dance of Husbands in Bathrobes

From the windows of the house
at the top of the hill
comes a stately music;
it is the funeral lament of Palestrina,
mourning his first wife
now that he is about
to take a second, a wealthy widow.

Men shuffle from doorways
half-asleep; it is the Dance
of Husbands in Bathrobes.
They have something to say
with their slipper-shod feet,
their awkward hands,
unready for the day's work,
their thin, disorderly hair,
but they do not know what it is.

They advance, pick up the morning paper,
turn this way and that.
Wives and children rush to the window
to gasp and applaud
as the husbands leap higher and higher,
dancing and weeping—
the sun is breaking their hearts!
Look, look, they are sinking into
such sorrow as only happy men can know.

Dracula in Las Vegas

As Dracula is killing the pimps of Las Vegas,
begging them not to sell their sisters into bondage,
then flying into a rage and tearing their throats out

when they laugh at him and call him a jive chump,
Elvis is crawling out of the penthouse window
at the Hilton International. Tonight he is going

to make his stand before the over-thirty crowd:
pacing back and forth like a cat-footed killer,
he is going to give them all he's got,

then wipe the sweat from his face with scarves
and fling them into the audience, but right now
he is crawling down the side of the Hilton head first,

wrapped in a red monk's robe over black nylon pajamas
and patent leather boots, his eyes screened
by tinted aviator glasses with the initials "EP"

across the bridge. He reaches the sidewalk
and lands lightly on his feet just as Dracula
steps forward and raises a hand as if to say, Stop.

Aaahunnnnghhh! cries Elvis, like a mountain lion
with an arrow in his ribs, as behind him appear
the dead of the desert: the naked Paiute Indians

who bet their wives on the toss of a stick,
the horse soldiers in blue, their skin hanging
from their faces, the Mormons who slaughtered

gentle immigrants from Arkansas on the strength
of a revelation. Dracula shakes his head:
I see you are afraid to face me alone, he says.

Ah've got to have mah power! Elvis snarls.
Ah've got to have mah dynamics!
You lounge lizard, says the sanguinary count,

whatever happened to my Transylvania Twist?
Elvis screams and writhes like a man in flames;
the monk's robe changes color, becomes light blue

and vaporous, like the screens of millions
of television sets on Sunday night when America
sat down in a body to watch Ed Sullivan

wring his hands and bring out Elvis in his prime
along with Lesley Gore, the Doodletown Pipers,
Gary Lewis and the Playboys, and Mary Hopkin singing

"Those Were the Days," then bluer still
as it gathers at the legs and waist, settling over
the shoulders like a jacket from which someone

has forgotten to remove the hanger, the lapels
as lumpy as cold gravy, the suit as blue now as the jowls
of former U.S. President Richard M. Nixon,

whose head floats where Elvis's did,
the eyes wide, the lips silently mouthing the words
I am not a crook then freezing in an inaudible scream

as the dead of the desert burst into laughter
and melt dervish-like into the first rays of the sun.
Something stirs at Dracula's feet: a green shoot,

then another, and another. A carpet of grass
rolls across the desert, a tide of vegetation
broken here and there by shade trees and pools

where the chorines and croupiers bathe, the call girls,
the mobsters come down from their meathooks,
all children again, children in the slowly warming air.

Dining with the Children of Krishna

The Krishna people have invited me
to dinner at a house on the gulf.
Getting out of my car, I see myself
in the window, a slightly paunchy man
who parts his hair on the left side.
In the house, the Krishna men are slim
and have topknots. The Krishna women
wear saris and are called "mother,"
but they do not look like my mother.
They defer to the men. The men
speak occasionally, but they do not
interrupt the Spiritual Master;
the women do not speak at all.

The Spiritual Master is more like me
than anyone else in the room:
we are close in age, and he spends
much of his time translating poetry.
When a devotee asks him what he thinks
of the conflict in the Middle East,
he blinks and stares at her in surprise.
I try to tell him what is important
to people like me, to see things clearly
and be kind to others, but the Spiritual
Master says, having gone that far,
why not go further and attain
the Absolute, the source from which
all kindness, all clarity flow?

A meal is served: it is the most
delicious food I have ever had
in my life. In another room,
someone plays a raga; the music is beautiful,
just as the Krishna people are pleasant if,

with the exception of the Spiritual Master,
bland. It is then that I say to myself
yes, I want to go to heaven.
I want to go to a place where,
solitary, grumpy, ill-fed,
the people do not know what they believe.

After Midnight

From the heart of this
house come sounds, the
soft bump of a receiver,
the almost noiseless swish
of the cord against the
wall: someone is hanging
up the phone in the
kitchen. Yet you are
asleep, your nightgown
bunched around your waist,
and we are alone, or
should be, and I am afraid,
though not for us.
I think it must be
someone who is in great
danger. I think it must
be someone made crazy
by pain. I think it
must be someone who
has been wandering from
yard to yard and is now
in our kitchen, calling
people in other cities,
other countries, other
worlds, saying *a child is
missing* or *everyone is
dead in there* or *I don't
love you anymore*.

Revenge

I think of my enemies
and, in a moment of weakness,
summon the forces of Imperial Japan.

Later I will regret this,
but now it is too late to stop them,
for having breakfasted

on black tea, rice, and pickles,
having listened to a fiery speech
by Foreign Minister Matsuoka,

the celebrated Talking Machine,
Mr. 50,000 Words, they move forward,
led by the Nine Young Men of Niigata,

who were so willing to die
that they sent their own nine fingers
in a jar of alcohol.

There are hundreds of soldiers now,
each wearing the hachimaki headband
and the belt into which his mother

has woven a thousand prayers
for good luck and a good fight.
At first they are joking,

saying "Don't miss the bus!"
and jostling each other,
but before long their eyes are bright

and they are shouting, "Sleep on kindling,
lick gall!" and "We must have courage
to do extraordinary things—

like jumping, with eyes closed,
off the verandah of the Kiyomizu Temple!"
Now they are running

in full banzai formation,
tens of thousands of khaki-clad men
flashing bayonets, swords, battle flags,

screaming "Punishment of Heaven!"
or simply "Wah! Charge!"
as the Kaiten human torpedoes

tunnel through the azaleas
and, overhead, the Iron Typhoon!
the Heavenly Wind!

the White Chrysanthemum bombers
falling, falling, as I urge them on
in my cocked hat, plumes, braids,

decorations, my gold-headed cane
pounding the ground,
my voice rising shrilly

in a jackhammer stutter,
screaming Suck on this,
you sons of b-bitches, you bastards!

Fallen Bodies

The night of the Franklinton game
the bus breaks down, the seniors cry
because they will never play football again,
and we all go home with our parents and girlfriends.
Billy Berry lies in the back of my father's Buick,
covered with bruises, unable to lift his right arm,
and tells stories he swears are true:

that apple seeds cure cancer,
that a giant dove hovered over the van
the night his church group
came back from Mexico,
that Hitler left Germany by submarine
after the war and established a haven
in Queen Maud Land, near the South Pole.

The air comes in through windows
that won't quite close
as we drive up the dark highway to Baton Rouge,
through towns where tired old men
sell peaches on the corners of used car lots
or doze in diners that sag by the roadside,
spacecraft cooling in the Louisiana night.

Theology from the Viewpoint of a Younger Son

My younger son, still in kindergarten,
wants to know how Jesus died.
I give him the biblical version,
but talk of scourging and crucifixion
only confuses him, and finally he says,
"I thought he was fooling around with a knife."
If that were the case, I say,
the New Testament would be another story altogether,
and the magnificent cathedrals of Europe
would be so different,
the crosses over the altar
replaced with great shiny blades. . . .

Listen, you little heresiarch,
you're not the first comedian in church history.
Take St. Martin: the crippled beggars
of Touraine took flight at the approach
of his miraculous corpse, fearing the saint
would heal and thus impoverish them,
which he did anyway, just to teach them a lesson.
Or St. Brendan the Navigator, who made camp
on the back of a whale, discovering his mistake
only after he had lit a fire for supper.

The devil is grim, he does not laugh,
but we do. It's not easy, being a younger son,
having so many masters. "We too must write bibles,"
says Emerson. Besides, the world is so stupid.
No amount of explanation is sufficient, sonny.
You're right: he was fooling around with a knife.

Love in the Flower of Chong

I am sitting in the Flower of Chong,
waiting for my order to arrive
and wondering
how the Chinese fall in love
if, as it is said,
they all look alike.
My own waiter
has shiny black hair
and eyes the shape of almonds,
but so do all the others.
Yet I am sure
his sweetheart is
no less passionate than my own.

I am about to decide
that love has a spiritual dimension
when my waiter appears
holding a platter
of Wind-Dry Sausage With Raw Lettuce,
and yes, I see now
that he is different
from the other waiters
in a hundred ways,
that he is someone I could pick out
not only in a half-empty Soho restaurant
but in the great market square
of Beijing itself,

only now he is casting about
in despair,
peering into the face
of one customer after another,
each of us the same.

Catholic Boys

At Sacred Heart, if you said you did it,
the priests shouted aloud
and people twisted in their pews
to see who left the little black booth;

once, at Our Lady of Mercy,
Father Becnel dragged Michael Kadair
into the aisle and told him
never to come back, and we wondered
if Mike had confessed to a new grip
or if Father had caught him at it

then and there. The priests raved on,
drunk with fury; nothing fell off
but our faith. Still, to disobey
is painful. We turned serious and pale
and spoke only among ourselves,
and our mothers wept.

Then Eddie Graham saved our souls:
Go to St. Mary's, he said one day,
the priests there have heard everything.
We went, and it was true. God forgave us,
and we took the sacraments again.

Now I am a grown man and a skeptic.
I have a lovely wife.

Beets

I pass over them in the cafeteria,
and at the homes of friends,
I eat around them.
I have always eaten around them.

Oh, you take your asparagus,
your oysters, your single-malt whiskey:
these we love because they are so different.

but the juice of the beet
is blood-red and sweet,

and once, when I bit one, long ago,
it resisted, then split softly,
like some unnecessary part of myself
that had been boiled
and left to cool,
unwanted, alone,
deserving no better fate.

The Society of Animals

I am denied it,
or at least that
of the animals I would have around me,
the hairy and four-legged,
the dog who sheds,
the cat with its tenacious dander,
arrow-shaped under the microscope
and fatal, at least to me.

The wild ones mark off
their proper fiefs.
The timberwolf sprays its potent piss,
the solitary hippo leaves
mounds of loamy spinach
at the corners of its domain,
but I am thrust
into a territory I have not chosen
without so much as a bird—too dusty
and prone to mites.

They will not have me,
none save Joey the Turtle,
who swims to the edge of his tank,
belly pale and vulnerable,
to bring me his,
the least objectionable love.

The Example of Nuns)

When I was six
I wanted to be chaste
like the nuns in *Life* magazine,
breasting the waves
in their thick cotton habits,
so that when death came
it would be as a mist,
a swirling bank of love
so marvellous that even
a six-year-old would say,
"Quick, take me
before anyone sees!"
Now it is late,
and I am old.
Today the nuns in El Salvador
stood in the way
when soldiers began
to herd the peasants
onto trucks;
they smiled and waved
at the TV cameras
and threatened to phone
the ambassador.
Once again I vow
to enjoy myself
and be good.

Complicity

On ne parle pas du corde
dans la maison du pendu.
                    —traditional French saying

A dog kills a chicken
on the farm where I am born,
and my mother ties the dead bird
to his collar. The dog looks sorry
for a day or two; the chicken,
rank and muddy, is taken away
and burned. And I, who feed
both dogs and chickens, wonder
if I will ever have to face the world
with my sins around my neck.

These days I have no dog,
and the only chickens I see
are in restaurants. I eat them
with potatoes and green peas,
and when the waiter whispers,
"Each of us has done something terrible,"
I ask him to be please, be quiet
before the other customers hear:
one should not speak of rope
in the house of the hanged.

⁂ The Very Rich Hours of the Houses of France

Our plane falls from the sky
into France, where everyone seems
so much happier than we are,
but no, it is not the people
who are happy, it is the buildings,
the high-beamed Norman farmhouses,
the cottages with roofs of trim thatch,
the châteaux set in verdant vineyards.
The people are like you and me:
their clothes don't fit very well,
their children are ungrateful,
and they're always blowing their noses.
But the buildings are warm and well-lit,
and even the ones that aren't,
the ones that have bad lighting
and poor insulation and green things
growing on the tile, even these
seem to be trying like crazy to comfort us,
to say something to us in French,
in House, in words we can understand.

Patience

His first marriage annulled due to chronic impotence
(though he could masturbate, he said, telling his friends
he had become another Rousseau), he puts it aside forever:

the loneliness, the desire to have someone to come home to,
to take tea with, someone to *see*, then the meeting with Effie Gray,
the courtship and engagement, the long ride after the ceremony,

she with her period, he with a bad cold. Worse, there was the hair:
Ruskin had seen it in pictures of naked bawds, but a wife
should be as white and smooth as a statue, he thinks.

They put off consummation, agree to it, put it off again,
associating the act with babies, whom Ruskin finds too small,
until Effie ends the marriage, later entering into

a conventionally happy union with the painter John Everett Millais
as Ruskin finds his head turned increasingly
by the thirteen-year-old Irish girl Rose La Touche,

whom he is to court by letter.
Getting no satisfactory reply, he seeks messages
from her through random openings of the Bible,

dreams of her, sees her name hidden within other names, carries
with him one of her own poor letters between thin sheets of gold
and offers it to her at a chance meeting in the Royal Academy.

Rose, now anorectic and soon to die, says "no" as he offers
the gold-wrapped letter, "no, Mr. Ruskin," again and again.
Seven years later he finds that he cannot stop thinking of her.

One night he flees Oxford for an inn in Abingdon
where he leaves the door open and, on returning,
sees that the wind has blown the melting candle wax

into the shape of the letter "R."
Beginning a new cycle of hope and despair,
he journeys to Venice, where he takes as gondolier

a horrid monster with inflamed eyes as red as coals
and, setting out for the Convent of the Armenians,
becomes lost in the fog, landing at the madhouse on the island

of San Clemente. There he waits for something, anything,
a voice from the outside. Suddenly there are fireflies!
The black water seems measureless as they flicker and reappear.

The Reason Why

If we were to let ourselves fall from time to time
and not always pull the world toward us,
it would take only the occasional misstep
to make us part of it all:
the *felix culpa*, the fall of the Friars Minor
from the high and beautiful tree
in which Brother James of Massa saw them,
the rise and fall of the Third Reich,
the jerk and buck of our own orgasm
as we seem to be lifted by the shoulders
and let suddenly down. Maybe
we should love this way always, like an idiot,
a drunk at poolside tumbling backward
into the water, dragging guests and waiters
with him. Maybe love alone can grab and hold
and be just, pull us under, let us go.

You Can't Always Get What You Want

A painter named Jules Holtzapfel blew out his brains in his studio in 1866 and in his suicide note declared: "The members of the jury have refused my work, therefore I am without talent . . . and must die!" But it is likely that Holtzapfel really was without talent.
    —F. W. J. HEMMINGS, *Culture and Society in France, 1848–1948*

The Rolling Stones were right:
You can't always get what you want.
This is true everywhere. For example,
early one Sunday morning last May,
on KPLM-TV in Palm Springs, California,
a man and woman coupled imaginatively
for eight minutes, then disappeared forever
into the electronic blizzard that blows
across "America," so named because
a German cartographer in Paris,
for reasons best known to himself,
decided to translate the first name
of Amerigo Vespucci into Latin.
Their demonstration of love and agility
never made it to the networks;
millions who learned of it later
were disappointed, and no wonder.
Talent, fame, a little sex on the weekend:
the things we really want are denied us,
and the rest we cannot explain.
Like the old mapmaker we are all Germans,
each of us lives in Paris,
Italian is what we translate,
Latin is what we write when we
think about countries we will never visit,
guess at what we will never know.

The Villa

First there are the wild trees,
the ones without name.
Then espaliered seedlings,
an allée lined with elms,
a grotto with sibyls in it,
a stair bordered by dry foundations,
a fish pool, dry,
stucco figures of fauns with a wineskin,
of a horse attacked by a lion,
and everywhere no sound,
not even birdsong,
though language
that expressed everything
was once spoken
in these gardens
by people who thought it
durable as stone.
They spoke it
until they could no longer
describe themselves.
They used it up,
and now the villa is empty
and hard to see
in the half-light,
but in the piano nobile
there are glimpses
of ancient landscapes,
of ruins above a bay of water,
of a round temple,
of someone watching—
no, there is a false door,
painted as if partially open,
and in it stands a man
in red hose and brown tunic

cradling a hunting cat on a chain,
its head turned toward a statue
in the foyer of a man
holding a woman by the waist,
and though her body is pressed
against him as in love,
she is looking over her shoulder
at something he cannot see.
In a tapestry, women sitting on a brocade
are conversing with a deer,
while behind them
a knight beseeches a demoiselle
who is turning into a tree;
he begs her, he implores,
but already there is
a look on her face
that speaks without speaking,
that says soon you too will be silent.

Looking for the Poem
That Explains It All

Someday I hope to find the poem
that tells me what is wrong
with everybody, why the beautiful
young girls in horror movies
turn to hags whose skin drips
from their faces, for instance,
or why people drive down the street
with looks of unbearable smugness,
as if to say, "My kids are better
than your kids, they will grow up
to be doctors and lawyers,
and I will always drive this big,
expensive car," and all the while
their coat or skirt is hanging
out of the door, torn and greasy,
dragging the ground. Sometimes
I myself hang up the receivers
of pay phones and tickle
the coin return, a furtive, almost
sexual gesture, only nothing
ever comes out except, once,
a small octagonal coin with a hole
in the middle and markings
no one could understand.

Saving the Young Men of Vienna

How bad it was, how embarrassing, to have been a young man
(to take the young men only) in Freud's Vienna, to go
to prostitutes and get syphilis and gonorrhea
or masturbate and become neurasthenic and then impotent,
to marry and either give new wives these terrible diseases
or dangle before them helplessly, driving them mad.

And even if these young men (again, to take the young men only)
were to make their way through the snares and pitfalls
of sexual development without accident,
avoiding the scarring experiences that turn young men
into fetishists and inverts, still they would sink
to the pavement of Vienna, finally, in sheer Oedipal exhaustion.

Therefore how wonderful it was, how unarguably wonderful,
for Dr. Freud, not just an enormous intellect
but a genius, in fact, though a rather nervous man
in his own right, one so shy that he had to sit
behind these troubled fellows so that he would not have
to be stared at all day long, to listen to their recitations

without directing his attention to anything in particular,
maintaining the same "evenly suspended attention"
in the face of all that he heard, allowing the patient
to drift without aim, without desire,
only interceding to help repetition become remembrance
as the patient surrendered his hysterical misery

and rose, pale and shaken but more certain
than ever before in his life, to go again
into the streets of Vienna and stroll about freely,
greeting old friends, pausing to buy a newspaper
or smoke a cigarette, doing precisely as he pleased,
embracing at last the common unhappiness.

Baths

Nearly all the Iliad *takes place far from hot baths. Nearly all of*
human life has always passed far from hot baths.

—SIMONE WEIL

Baths are one more thing
to be separate from:
the steam,
the sweet slick of soap,
the unhurried attention
to nail and crevice,
the water rising,
the wet hair.
The senses sleep and wake—
something tolls you back,
a word like a bell,
and you go
to whatever calls you
from this tub
to the next.
Distance itself is a bath:
the mind walks over white tile,
past wooden benches
and narrow doors,
and keeps walking.

Conversations with the Dead ☦

They are not lazy, the dead. They visit us in our sleep
and ask us to confess to crimes we never committed.
They remind us of our animal instincts, how we fought
to protect ourselves, how no one can blame us—
don't be afraid to say "I did it," they advise.
One minute they are so nice that we hope
we can live with them when all of this is over,
but when we do not say exactly what they want to hear,
they scream and threaten to lock us up like animals.
After a while we are tired and want to sleep again,
but they keep taking us back to the moment it all began,
the night the officer saw her lying there with her shirt
around her neck, or that cold morning when the mist rose
from the lake, and they pulled the car out of the water.

Firecracker

It is 1956. Bill Reilly and I
have just bought firecrackers,
and his father is chewing us out
over dinner. Only a dope
would burn up his money that way,
says his father as he lights a cigarette.

Then what does that make you,
says Bill, who is about to put
a big pot of spaghetti on the table.
Pow! The father swings, missing Bill
but not the pot. My mouth flies open:

there is spaghetti on the wall,
on the ceiling, in everyone's hair.
The Reilly sisters cry. Mrs. Reilly faints.
The knuckles on the father's hand
swell and turn gray as Bill charges out
into the yard, bellowing with terror,

and I turn to go. In the driveway I start to run
and then cheer as loudly as I can.
I run all the way home, stopping only
to piss in Old Man Kern's mailbox.
I am twelve years old and happy to be alive.

More Shrines

No, I don't think we would
be orthodox believers
had Charles Martel not
turned back the Moslems
at Tours in 732, thus
allowing the West to
grow up Christian, Jewish,
and, for the most part,
slightly perplexed about
but mainly oblivious to
such matters as good,
evil, and whether or not
we will go to Paradise
when we die. But even
though my hometown of
Tallahassee contains the
name of Allah, and even
though we have Arabic
words in our language,
such as algebra, which
sounds Arabic and even
looks that way, or did
in the eighth grade,
still, this is America,
and while I cannot see
us adopting the placid
temperaments of the
desert people, so
self-composed in their
long, loose robes yet
struggling continuously
with the malicious *djinn*
who rule the kingdom of
death that begins just

a few feet from the oasis,
we need, do we not, more
places in this country
that are solemn and
serene, although there
can be only one holy
stone set in the corner
of the Ka'aba in Mecca,
white when given to Adam
at the time of the fall but
black now from the sins
of those who have kissed it.
I like this: a kind
of sin-magnet that
would pull all of the
wickedness out of us,
because, as it says
in the Koran, you
can run, pretty momma,
but you can't hide.

The Wanderer

I am strolling through the mall,
minding my own business,
when a small, sad-eyed man

crooks his finger
and beckons me over
to a makeshift booth

where he tries to sell me a product
that will keep mist from forming
on my bathroom mirror.

For me, this is not a problem,
I tell him: when mist forms
on my bathroom mirror,

I just wipe it off with my hand.
He offers to lower the price,
and I say that mist

on the bathroom mirror at my house
will never be a problem,
no matter how cheap the product.

He looks at me as though I am crazy,
and for a moment I can see
all the things that must worry this man:

that people in South America
are not flossing their teeth;
that a woman in Milan

will flush a sanitary napkin
down ancient plumbing;
that somewhere, a child

with murder in his face
is about to tear the health department tag
off his brand-new mattress.

This sad-eyed man is the one
who worries about the small things;
he looks old, and I imagine him

plodding across the parched sand
of Arabia Deserta. In the cities
men are killing each other,

but he continues patiently
in the white martyrdom of his exile,
looking for something

new to worry about, something small.
At home I shower and shave
and start to wipe the mist

from my bathroom mirror
when I freeze, afraid that
he has followed me,

that he has gotten into my house,
that I will see his face
looking over my shoulder.

I stare out
at myself, wide-eyed
and forever trivial.

Myopia

It is eleven years ago,
and the truth is about to be
revealed to someone
who will not understand it—
me, who is sitting
in the little train station
at Pompeii, holding my infant son,
who has just peed in his pants.
His mother and I have quarreled,
and she is slow to return
from the city of the dead.
It is cold,
and my son's dampness
has spread through my overcoat
and sweater to my skin.
On the shelf in the station
there are souvenirs,
including busts of John F. Kennedy,
who is popular the world over,
and Mussolini.
If there is a connection
between these two men,
I do not get it.

Years later, I learn
that the American president
was more interested in women
than in the affairs of state.
One of his paramours says,
in a magazine interview,
"He was as compulsive as Mussolini:
up against the wall, signora,
if you have five minutes,

that sort of thing."
The horniness of our leaders
disgusts me. In Italy
they may do as they please,
but the business of America
is not monkey business.
My son is nearly twelve now;
he makes A's in school and
has not peed in his pants for years.
His mother and I are divorced.
I have remarried
and would like to take
my new wife to Pompeii,
city of oracles.

What Can You Do?

Say it was just after
something terrible had
happened—a city burned,
the bottom fell out
of the market, there was
a war and the wrong side
won—and someone was
just sitting down to
eat a ham, say, or a pie,
when along comes somebody
else, the kind of person
who hopes that something
terrible will happen
so he can smile through
it all and have people
say isn't he wonderful
and oh, how brave,
only now he is standing
over the person with the
food, saying how can you
eat at a time like this?
Say that happened, then.
And now say that a man
does his woman wrong,
or someone gives
somebody else a dirty
deal. Then it would
seem right for a friend

or a relative to be
there, saying how can
you eat when things
are not the way they
should be? Or you do it.
You call them up and say
look, put down that fork,
this is serious.

Repression

I rather think
I believe in it,
in the need
to keep things in
until our eyes are red
with desire or rage,
then lash ourselves
until we faint with pain
or build bridges.
I was repressing something
just the other day,
as a matter of fact,
a childhood memory:
it must have been
the time my parents
gave away some of my toys
because I wasn't playing
with them anymore.
They certainly looked
desirable as my father
pitched them into
the Goodwill bin,
I can tell you that!
Thus do we spend our days:
a man gazing fondly
at his wife's *mons*
will begin to wonder
if it looks more like
the face of Sigmund Freud,
Karl Marx, or Joseph Conrad,
when what he should do
is embrace her;
afterwards he can engage
in self-study and ask himself

what kind of person
would emerge were he
to lose all his inhibitions.
And would his wife
continue to love him?
Almost certainly not,
but that would depend
on how deeply she looked:
in a notebook
Hawthorne describes an allegory
he wanted to write
but never did;
in it the Heart
is sunny around its Portals,
then sinister just inside,
which is about as far
as anyone ever goes,
but at its core,
a Garden.

Money Is Falling Out of Our Mouths

As Dostoevsky said,
one sacred memory
from childhood
is perhaps
the best education of all.

Maybe that's what
my son was talking about
when he glanced around
at dinner the other night
and whispered,
"We look like millionaires."

Once I overheard
my mother murmuring
to my father,
and I asked her
what she had said;

she blushed
and looked at the ground
and asked,
"Can't a husband
and wife have secrets?"

Husband! *Wife*!
How those words burned me!
In that moment
I lost the power of speech,
and it was years
before I got it back.

Fear of Reading

I have just finished one novel
and am picking up another
reluctantly, because
I do not want to crowd
two sets of characters
together, to have
the Duchesse de Guermantes
sitting down to dinner with
Rodion Romanovitch Raskolnikov
or Huck and Jim trying
to keep up with Leopold Bloom
as he makes his way
through the streets of Dublin.

At times, art is too much for me.
Once the composer Ives
said to a fellow who was booing him,
"Stop being such a God-damned sissy!
Why can't you stand up before
fine strong music like this
and use your ears like a man!"

I am a sissy, though.
I walked around in a daze
before I read Henry James;
afterwards, it all made sense.
That is why I am afraid of books:
they have saved my life before,
surely they could kill me.

Correction

In my newspaper
there is a feature
called "Setting It Straight,"
which points out that,
for example, the second paragraph
in last Tuesday's article
about the mayor's brother's accident
should have contained the phrase
"traveled twenty feet
before landing unhurt
in a swimming pool."
By this time,
no one can remember
what the article said
and therefore no one knows
who went through the air,
whether it was the brother
or the mayor himself
or someone wholly unconnected
to either of them,
a person who just rose
into the air miraculously
at about the time
the mayor's brother drove by.
Or maybe this is the real news,
what we explain to ourselves.

Legacy

Our ancestors leave too much:
habits, reason, their own deaths.
We long to be excited all the time.
Last night at the Tonhalle
the musicians smashed their instruments,
and this morning I woke with a headache;
when I opened the dictionary
there were more words in it
than ever before.

Still, at any moment I could step out
of this house, which I know so well,
and listen as the birds
grow silent in the trees.
One day I will be like them.
And one day you will be like me
unless I leave you nothing,
not even my memory,
not even this poem.

Russia

A woman lifts a wine bottle
and brings it down
on the head of her lover,
who falls dead at her feet.

At the trial a student
leaps up, pale with love,
and says he did it,
so they take him away.

When he gets out of prison,
he goes down to the river,
where he sees the woman
reading under a tree.

She has become
a young girl again.
He offers her a bouquet
and says marry me, marry me

but she throws the flowers
in the water and says nothing.
It is the most beautiful
day of his life.

Unnatural Acts

"Yes," she said, "he got female students in his office
and exposed himself to them. But that's over now—
he left town." Which is what they always say:

he went away, poor guy, he left town, he had to leave.
But where do they go, these flashers, frotteurs,
and sniffers of girls' bicycle seats?

Is there a town for nonviolent sex offenders
just north of the state line, like the leper colony
at Carville or Thomas Mann's sanatorium?

I see it clearly: tract houses behind a high fence,
clean streets and sidewalks, children playing
contentedly, busy wives running errands,

and everywhere these men, still pale and intent
but happier now as they help the elderly cross streets,
hawk light bulbs and brooms door to door

for charitable causes, do yardwork for the infirm,
rescue cats from trees, involve themselves
in all manner of strange, deviant behavior.

Transmutation as a Fact of Life

Forget the mysteries of mineral prudence,
the chemical weddings, the sympathetic
powders that cure wounds at a distance,
the stone at the heart of the Alchemical
Citadel, guarded by a dragon, attainable only
by the silent, the faithful, the pure of heart—
it is enough to know that when Albertus Magnus
gave a dinner for the Count of Holland,
the table was set in the snow-covered garden
of the monastery, and as the startled guests
took their places, warm breezes blew, and
spring flowers pushed up through the frozen earth.

Oh, Ko Hung of China, Thrice-Great Hermes,
do rocks not copulate, give birth, and die?
Strike me with iron tempered
in the urine of a small, red-headed boy
if we are not, all of us,
trying to do something about the weather.

Mothers and Fathers

In old photographs they are dark-browed,
their eyes set deeply in faces shadowed
by the brims of hats no longer fashionable.
The years go by; they become lighter
and, finally, white. Each day they are
more and more transparent, and soon
we shall not be able to see them at all.
Oh, we shall hear the rustle of clothing
in other rooms, but when we look,
no one will be there; the phone will ring,
but when we pick it up, no one will answer.
At the last minute they will appear again,
and we shall reach for them,
but the wind will blow them away,
like the hollow, stemlike scapes of the
dandelion, floating forever on the dry air.

The Cows Are Going to Paris: A Pastoral

The cows are going to Paris;
when they boarded the train
at Corbeil and Fontainebleau
the people were frightened
and ran out into the fields and meadows
and chewed the grass in terror,

and now the cows are going to
shop at the Galeries Lafayette,
stroll in the Louvre and the Jeu de Paume,
see plays produced and directed by cows,
a farce in the manner
of Georges Feydeau, for example,

in which a certain Monsieur Bull
wishes to deceive his wife,
so he arranges to meet the wife
of a friend in a hotel of low repute.
The only one who can betray him
is another monsieur who stutters

whenever it rains.
And of course it rains:
"M-m-mooo!" he says, "M-m-m-moooo!"
The cows are delighted;
they have never thought of the rain
as having so much meaning until now.

And when the deceived monsieur
grabs a sword in order to
pierce the innards of his false friend,
the cows are absolutely enthralled,
it having never occurred to them
that the slaughter of their species

could be occasioned by anything
other than the desire to eat
or make money, that it could have
rage as its cause,
a feeling of betrayal,
the breaking of a heart.

Meanwhile, the people from the train
have made themselves comfortable
under the trees;
the diet of the cows
is nourishing and unrefined,

and somehow it seems natural
to stand in small groups for hours,
saying nothing. Indeed,
when the cows return
to the fields and meadows,

the people will not get back on board
and must be prodded
before they enter the cars.
Having been to the city, the cows understand;
to them, the people are like

the nymphs and shepherds in the painting
by Watteau who are made to leave
the isle of forgetfulness and so set out
for the fallen world, but slowly,
and not without a mournful backward glance.

DESIGNED BY HERBERT JOHNSON
COMPOSED BY POLEBRIDGE PRESS, SONOMA, CALIFORNIA
MANUFACTURED BY THOMSON-SHORE, INC., DEXTER, MICHIGAN
TEXT AND DISPLAY LINES ARE SET IN GALLIARD

Library of Congress Cataloging-in-Publication Data
Kirby, David K.
Saving the young men of Vienna.
(The Brittingham prize in poetry)
I. Title. II. Series.
PS3561.I66S4   1987   811'.54   87–40148
ISBN 0–299–11220–9
ISBN 0–299–11224–1 (pbk.)